Kristen Suzanne's
EASY
Raw Vegan
Desserts

Delicious & Easy Raw Food Recipes
for Cookies, Pies, Cakes,
Puddings, Mousses, Cobblers,
Candies & Ice Creams

by Kristen Suzanne

*Green
Butterfly
Press*

Scottsdale, Arizona

OTHER BOOKS BY KRISTEN SUZANNE

- *Kristen's Raw: The EASY Way to Get Started & Succeed at the Raw Food Vegan Diet & Lifestyle*
- *Kristen Suzanne's EASY Raw Vegan Entrees*
- *Kristen Suzanne's EASY Raw Vegan Soups*
- *Kristen Suzanne's EASY Raw Vegan Salads & Dressings*
- *Kristen Suzanne's EASY Raw Vegan Sides & Snacks*
- *Kristen Suzanne's EASY Raw Vegan Smoothies, Juices, Elixirs & Drinks (includes wine drinks!)*
- *Kristen Suzanne's EASY Raw Holidays*
- *Kristen Suzanne's EASY Raw Vegan Dehydrating*
- *Kristen Suzanne's Ultimate Raw Vegan Hemp Recipes*

COMING SOON

- *Kristen Suzanne's Raw Vegan Diet for EASY Weight Loss*
- *Kristen Suzanne's Ultimate Raw Vegan Chocolate Recipes*

For details, Raw Food resources, and Kristen's free Raw Food newsletter, please visit:

KristensRaw.com

For information on excerpting, reprinting or licensing portions of this book, please write to info@greenbutterflypress.com.

Green Butterfly Press
19550 N. Gray Hawk Drive, Suite 1042
Scottsdale, AZ 85255 USA

Library of Congress Control Number: 2008941402
Library of Congress Subject Heading:
1. Cookery (Natural foods) 2. Raw foods

ISBN: 978-0-9817556-1-8
1.2

CONTENTS

CHAPTER 1

RAW BASICS

NOTE: "Raw Basics" is a brief introduction to Raw for those who are new to the subject. It is the same in all of my recipe books. If you have recently read this section in one of them, you may wish to skip to Chapter 2.

WHY RAW?

Living the Raw vegan lifestyle has made me a more effective person... in everything I do. I get to experience pure, sustainable all-day-long energy. My body is in perfect shape and I gain strength and endurance in my exercise routine with each passing day. My relationships are the best they've ever been, because I'm happy and I love myself and my life. My headaches have ceased to exist, and my skin glows with the radiance of brand new life, which is exactly how I feel. Raw vegan is the best thing that has ever happened to me.

Whatever your passion is in life (family, business, exercise, meditation, hobbies, etc.), eating Raw vegan will take it to unbelievable new heights. Raw vegan food offers you the most amazing benefits—physically, mentally, and spiritually. It is *the* ideal choice for your food consumption if you want to become the healthiest and best "you" possible. Raw vegan food is for people who want to live longer while feeling younger. It's for people who want to feel vibrant and alive, and want to enjoy life like never before. All I ever have to say to someone is, "Just try it for yourself." It will change your life. From simple to gourmet, there's always something for everyone, and it's delicious. Come into the world of Raw with me, and experience for yourself the most amazing health *ever*.

Are you ready for your new lease on life? The time is now. Let's get started!

SOME GREAT THINGS TO KNOW BEFORE DIVING INTO THESE RECIPES

Organic Food

I use organic produce and products for pretty much everything. There are very few exceptions, and that would be if the recipe called for something I just can't get organic such as jicama, young Thai coconuts, certain seasonings, or any random ingredient that my local health food store is not able to procure from an organic grower for whatever reason.

If you think organic foods are too expensive, then start in baby steps and buy a few things at a time. Realize that you're going to be spending less money in the long run on health problems as your health improves, and going organic is one way to facilitate that. I find that once people learn about the direct cause-and-effect relationship between non-organic food and illnesses such as cancer, the relatively small premium you pay for organic becomes a trivial non-issue. Your health is worth it!

Choosing organically grown foods is one of the most important choices we can make. The more people who choose organic, the lower the prices will be in the long run. Vote with your dollar! Here is something I do to help further this cause and you can, too... whenever I eat at a restaurant I always write on the bill, "I would eat here more if you served organic food." Can you imagine what would happen if we all did this?

It's essential to use organic ingredients for many reasons:

1. The health benefits – superior nutrition, reduced intake of chemicals and heavy metals and decreased exposure to carcinogens. Organic food has been shown to have up to 300% more nutrition than conventionally grown, non-organic produce.

2. To have the very best tasting food ever! I've had people tell me in my classes that they never knew vegetables tasted so good – and it's because I only use organic.

3. Greater variety of heirloom fruits and vegetables.

4. Cleaner rivers and waterways for our earth, along with minimized topsoil erosion.

Going Organic on a Budget:

Going organic on a budget is not impossible. Here are things to keep in mind that will help you afford it:

1. Buy in bulk. Ask the store you frequent if they'll give you a deal for buying certain foods by the case. (Just make sure it's a case of something that you can go through in a timely fashion so it doesn't go to waste). Consider this for bananas or greens especially if you drink lots of smoothies or green juice, like I do.

2. See if local neighbors, family or friends will share the price of getting cases of certain foods. When you do this, you can go beyond your local grocery store and contact great places (which deliver nationally) such as Boxed Greens (BoxedGreens.com) or Diamond Organics (DiamondOrganics.com). Maybe they'll extend a discount if your order goes above a certain

amount or if you get certain foods by the case. It never hurts to ask.

3. Pay attention to organic foods that are not very expensive to buy relative to the conventional prices (bananas, for example). Load up on those.

4. Be smart when picking what you buy as organic. Some conventionally grown foods have higher levels of pesticides than others. For those, go organic. Then, for foods that are not sprayed as much, you can go conventional. Avocados, for example, aren't sprayed too heavily so you could buy those as conventional. Here is a resource that keeps an updated list:

   foodnews.org/walletguide.php

5. Buy produce that is on sale. Pay attention to which organic foods are on sale for the week and plan your menu around that. Every little bit adds up!

6. Grow your own sprouts. Load up on these for salads, soups, and smoothies. Very inexpensive. Buy the organic seeds in the bulk bins at your health food store or buy online and grow them yourself. Fun!

7. Buy organic seeds/nuts in bulk online and freeze. Nuts and seeds typically get less expensive when you order in bulk from somewhere like Sun Organic (SunOrganic.com). Take advantage of this and freeze them (they'll last the year!). Do the same with dried fruits/dates/etc. And remember, when you make a recipe that calls for expensive nuts, you can often easily replace them with a less expensive seed such as sunflower or pumpkin seeds.

8. Buy seasonally; hence, don't buy a bunch of organic berries out of season (i.e., eat more apples and bananas in the fall and winter). Also, consider buying frozen organic fruits, especially when they're on sale!

9. Be content with minimal variety. Organic spinach banana smoothies are inexpensive. So, having this most mornings for your breakfast can save you money. You can change it up for fun by adding cinnamon one day, nutmeg another, vanilla extract yet another. Another inexpensive meal or snack is a spinach apple smoothie. Throw in a date or some raisins for extra pizazz. It helps the budget when you make salads, smoothies, and soups with ingredients that tend to be less expensive such as carrots (year round), bananas (year round), zucchini and cucumbers (in the summer), etc.

Kristen Suzanne's Tip: A Note About Herbs

Hands down, fresh herbs taste the best and have the highest nutritional value. While I recommend fresh herbs whenever possible, you can substitute dried herbs if necessary. But do so in a ratio of:

3 parts fresh to 1 part dried

Dried herbs impart a more concentrated flavor, which is why you need less of them. For instance, if your recipe calls for three tablespoons of fresh basil, you'll be fine if you use one tablespoon of dried basil instead.

The Infamous Salt Question: What Kind Do I Use?

All life on earth began in the oceans, so it's no surprise that organisms' cellular fluids chemically resemble sea water. Saltwater in the ocean is "salty" due to many, many minerals, not just sodium chloride. We need these minerals, not coincidentally, in roughly the same proportion that they exist in... guess where?... the ocean! (You've just gotta love Mother Nature.)

So when preparing food, I always use sea salt, which can be found at any health food store. Better still is sea salt that was deposited into salt beds before the industrial revolution started spewing toxins into the world's waterways. My personal preference is Himalayan Crystal Salt, fine granules. It's mined high in the mountains from ancient sea-beds, has a beautiful pink color, and imparts more than 84 essential minerals into your diet. You can use either the Himalayan crystal variety or Celtic Sea Salt, but I would highly recommend sticking to at least one of these two. You can buy Himalayan crystal salt through KristensRaw.com/store.

Kristen Suzanne's Tip: Start Small with Strong Flavors

FLAVORS AND THEIR STRENGTH

There are certain flavors and ingredients that are particularly strong, such as garlic, ginger, onion, and salt. It's important to observe patience here, as these are flavors that can be loved or considered offensive, depending on who is eating the food. I know people who want the maximum amount of salt called for in a recipe and I know some who are highly sensitive to it. Therefore, to make the best possible Raw experience for you, I recommend starting on the "small end" especially with ingredients like garlic, ginger, strong savory herbs and seasonings, onions (any variety), citrus, and even salt. If I've given you a range in a recipe, for instance *1/4 - 1/2 teaspoon Himalayan crystal salt* then I recommend starting with the smaller amount, and then tasting it. If you don't love it, then add a little more of that ingredient and taste it again. Start small. It's worth the extra 60 seconds it might take you to do this. You might end up using less, saving it for the next recipe you make and voila, you're saving a little money.

Lesson #1: It's very hard to correct any flavors of excess, so start small and build.

Lesson #2: Write it down. When an ingredient offers a "range" for itself, write down the amount you liked best. If you use an "optional" ingredient, make a note about that as well.

One more thing to know about some strong flavors like the ones mentioned above... with Raw food, these flavors can intensify the finished product as each day passes. For example, the garlic in your soup, on the day you made it, might be perfect. On day two, it's still really great but a little stronger in flavor. And by day three, you might want to carry around your toothbrush or a little chewing gum!

HERE IS A TIP TO HELP CONTROL THIS

If you're making a recipe in advance, such as a dressing or soup that you won't be eating until the following day or even the day after that, then hold off on adding some of the strong seasonings until the day you eat it (think garlic and ginger). Or, if you're going to make the dressing or soup in advance, use less of the strong seasoning, knowing that it might intensify on its own by the time you eat it. This isn't a huge deal because it doesn't change that dramatically, but I mention it so you won't be surprised, especially when serving a favorite dish to others.

Kristen Suzanne's Tip: Doubling Recipes

More often than not, there are certain ingredients and flavors that you don't typically double in their entirety, if you're making a double or triple batch of a recipe. These are strong-flavored ingredients similar to those mentioned above (salt, garlic, ginger, herbs, seasoning, etc). A good rule of thumb is this: For a double batch, use 1.5 times the amount for certain ingredients. Taste it and see if you need the rest. For instance, if I'm making a "double batch" of soup, and the normal recipe calls for 1 tablespoon of Himalayan crystal salt, then I'll put in 1 1/2 tablespoons to start, instead of two. Then, I'll taste it and add the remaining 1/2 tablespoon, if necessary.

This same principle is not necessarily followed when dividing a recipe in half. Go ahead and simply divide in half, or by whatever amount you're making. If there is a range for a particular ingredient provided, I still recommend that you use the smaller amount of an ingredient when dividing. Taste the final product and then decide whether or not to add more.

My recipes provide a variety of yields, as you'll see below. Some recipes make 2 servings and some make 4 - 6 servings. For those of you making food for only yourself, then simply cut the recipes making 4 - 6 servings in half. Or, as I always do... I make the larger serving size and then I have enough food for a couple of meals. If a recipe yields 2 servings, I usually double it for the same reason.

Kristen Suzanne's Tip: Changing Produce

"But I made it exactly like this last time! Why doesn't it taste the same?"

Here is something you need to embrace when preparing Raw vegan food. Fresh produce can vary in its composition of water, and even flavor, to some degree. There are times I've made marinara sauce and, to me, it was the perfect level of sweetness in the finished product. Then, the next time I made it, you would have thought I added a smidge of sweetener. This is due to the fact that fresh Raw produce can have a slightly different taste from time to time when you make a recipe (only ever so slightly, so don't be alarmed). *Aahhh, here is the silver lining!* This means you'll never get bored living the Raw vegan lifestyle because your recipes can change a little in flavor from time to time, even though you followed the same recipe. Embrace this natural aspect of produce and love it for everything that it is. ☺

This is much less of an issue with cooked food. Most of the water is taken out of cooked food, so you typically get the same flavors and experience each and every time. Boring!

Kristen Suzanne's Tip: Ripeness and Storage for Your Fresh Produce

1. I never use green bell peppers because they are not "ripe." This is why so many people have a hard time digesting them (often "belching" after eating them). To truly experience the greatest health, it's important to eat fruits and vegetables at their peak ripeness. Therefore, make sure you only use red, orange, or yellow bell peppers. Store these in your refrigerator.

2. A truly ripe banana has some brown freckles or spots on the peel. This is when you're supposed to eat a banana. Store these on your countertop away from other produce, because bananas give off a gas as they ripen, which will affect the ripening process of your other produce. And, if you have a lot of bananas, split them up. This will help prevent all of your bananas from ripening at once.

3. Keep avocados on the counter until they reach ripeness (when their skin is usually brown in color and if you gently squeeze it, it "gives" just a little). At this point, you can put them in the refrigerator where they'll last up to a week longer. If you keep ripe avocados on the counter, they'll only last another couple of days. Avocados, like bananas, give off a gas as they ripen, which will affect the ripening process of your other produce. Let them ripen away from your other produce. And, if you have a lot of avocados, separate them. This will help prevent all of your avocados from ripening at once.

4. Tomatoes are best stored on your counter. Do not put them in the refrigerator or they'll get a "mealy" texture.

5. Pineapple is ripe for eating when you can gently pull a leaf out of the top of it. Therefore, test your pineapple for ripeness at the store to ensure you're buying the sweetest one possible. Just pull one of the leaves out from the top. After 3 to 4 attempts on different leaves, if you can't gently take one of them out, then move on to another pineapple.

6. Stone fruits (fruits with pits, such as peaches, plums, and nectarines), bananas and avocados all continue to ripen after being picked.

7. I have produce ripening all over my house. Sounds silly maybe, but I don't want it crowded on my kitchen countertop. I move it around and turn it over daily.

For a more complete list of produce ripening tips, check out my book, *Kristen's Raw,* available at Amazon.com.

Kristen Suzanne's Tip: Proper Dehydration Techniques

Dehydrating your Raw vegan food at a low temperature is a technique that warms and dries the food while preserving its nutritional integrity. When using a dehydrator, it is recommended that you begin the dehydrating process at a temperature of 130 - 140 degrees for about an hour. Then, lower the temperature to 105 degrees for the remaining time of dehydration. Using a high temperature such as 140 degrees, *in the initial stages of dehydration,* does not destroy the nutritional value of the food. During this initial phase, the food does the most "sweating" (releasing moisture), which cools the food. Therefore, while the temperature of the air circulating *around* the food is about 140 degrees, the food itself is much cooler. These directions apply only when using an Excalibur Dehydrator because of their Horizontal-Airflow Drying System. Furthermore, I am happy to only recommend Excalibur dehydrators because of their first-class products and customer service. For details, visit the *Raw Kitchen Essential Tools* section of my website at KristensRaw.com/store.

MY YIELD AND SERVING AMOUNTS NOTED IN THE RECIPES

Each recipe in this book shows an approximate amount that the recipe yields (the quantity it makes). I find that "one serving" to me might be considered two servings to someone else, or vice versa. Therefore, I tried to use an "average" when listing the serving amount. Don't let that stop you from eating a two-serving dish in one sitting, if it seems like the right amount for you. It simply depends on how hungry you are.

WHAT IS THE DIFFERENCE BETWEEN CHOPPED, DICED, AND MINCED?

Chop

This gives relatively uniform cuts, but doesn't need to be perfectly neat or even. You'll often be asked to chop something before putting it into a blender or food processor, which is why it doesn't have to be uniform size since it'll be getting blended or pureed.

Dice

This produces a nice cube shape, and can be different sizes, depending on which you prefer. This is great for vegetables.

Mince

This produces an even, very fine cut, typically used for fresh herbs, onions, garlic and ginger.

Julienne

This is a fancy term for long, rectangular cuts.

WHAT EQUIPMENT DO I NEED FOR MY NEW RAW FOOD KITCHEN?

I go into much more detail regarding the perfect setup for your Raw vegan kitchen in my book, *Kristen's Raw,* which is a must read for anybody who wants to learn the easy ways to succeed with living the Raw vegan lifestyle. Here are the main pieces of equipment you'll want to get you going:

1. An excellent chef's knife (6 - 8 inches in length – non-serrated). Of everything you do with Raw food, you'll be chopping and cutting the most, so invest in a great knife. This truly makes doing all the chopping really fun!

2. Blender

3. Food Processor (get a 7 or 10-cup or more)

4. Juicer

5. Spiralizer or Turning Slicer

6. Dehydrator – Excalibur® is the best company by far and is available at KristensRaw.com

7. Salad spinner

8. Other knives (paring, serrated)

For links to online retailers that sell my favorite kitchen tools and foods, visit KristensRaw.com/store.

SOAKING AND DEHYDRATING NUTS AND SEEDS

This is an important topic. When using nuts and seeds in Raw vegan foods, you'll find that recipes sometimes call for them to be "soaked" or "soaked and dehydrated." Here is the low-down on the importance and the difference between the two.

Why should you soak your nuts and seeds?

Most nuts and seeds come packed by Mother Nature with enzyme inhibitors, rendering them harder to digest. These inhibitors essentially shut down the nuts' and seeds' metabolic activity, rendering them dormant—for as long as they need to be—until they detect a moisture-rich environment that's suitable for germination (e.g., rain). By soaking your nuts and seeds, you trick the nuts into "waking up," shutting off the inhibitors so that the enzymes can become active. This greatly enhances the nuts' digestibility for you and is highly recommended if you want to experience Raw vegan food in the healthiest way possible.

14

Even though you'll want to soak the nuts to activate their enzymes, before using them, you'll need to re-dry them and grind them down anywhere from coarse to fine (into a powder almost like flour), depending on the recipe. To dry them, you'll need a dehydrator. (If you don't own a dehydrator yet, then, if a recipe calls for "soaked and dehydrated," just skip the soaking part; you can use the nuts or seeds in the dry form that you bought them).

Drying your nuts (but not yet grinding them) is a great thing to do before storing them in the freezer or refrigerator (preferably in glass mason jars). They will last a long time and you'll always have them on hand, ready to use.

In my recipes, always use nuts and seeds that are "soaked and dehydrated" (that is, *dry*) unless otherwise stated as "soaked" (wet).

Some nuts and seeds don't have to follow the enzyme inhibitor rule; therefore, they don't need to be soaked. These are:

- Macadamia nuts
- Brazil nuts
- Pine nuts
- Hemp seeds
- Most cashews

An additional note... there are times when the recipe will call for soaking, even though it's for a type of nut or seed without enzyme inhibitors, such as Brazil nuts. The logic behind this is to help *soften* the nuts so they blend into a smoother texture, especially if you don't have a high-powered blender. This is helpful when making nut milks, soups and sauces.

Instructions for "Soaking" and "Soaking and Dehydrating" Nuts

"Soaking"

The general rule to follow: Any nuts or seeds that require soaking can be soaked overnight (6 - 10 hours). Put the required amount of nuts or seeds into a bowl and add enough water to cover by about an inch or so. Set them on your counter overnight. The following morning, or 6 - 10 hours after you soaked them, drain and rinse them. They are now ready to eat or use in a recipe. At this point, they need to be refrigerated in an airtight container (preferably a glass mason jar) and they'll have a shelf life of about 3 days maximum. Only soak the amount you're going to need or eat, unless you plan on dehydrating them right away.

A note about flax seeds and chia seeds... these don't need to be soaked if your recipe calls for grinding them into a powder. Some recipes will call to soak the seeds in their "whole-seed" form, before making crackers and bread, because they create a very gelatinous and binding texture when soaked. You can soak flax or chia seeds in a ratio of one-part seeds to two-parts water, and they can be soaked for as short as 1 hour and up to 12 hours. At this point, they are ready to use (don't drain them). Personally, when I use flax seeds, I usually grind them and don't soak them. It's hard for your body to digest "whole" flax seeds, even if they are soaked. It's much easier for your body to assimilate the nutrients when they're ground to a flax meal.

"Soaking and Dehydrating"

Follow the same directions for soaking. Then, after draining and rinsing the nuts, spread them out on a mesh dehydrator sheet and dehydrate them at 140 degrees for one hour. Lower the temperature to 105 degrees and dehydrate them until they're completely dry, which can take up to 24 hours.

Please note, all nuts and seeds called for in my recipes will always be "Raw and Organic" and "Soaked and Dehydrated" unless the recipe calls for soaking.

ALMOND PULP

Some of my recipes call for "almond pulp," which is really easy to make. After making your fresh almond milk (see "Nut Milk" recipe, below) and straining it through a "nut milk bag," (available at NaturalZing.com or you can use a paint strainer bag from the hardware store – much cheaper), you will find a nice, soft pulp inside the bag. Turn the bag inside out and flatten the pulp out onto a teflex dehydrator sheet with a spatula or your hand. Dehydrate the pulp at 140 degrees for one hour, then lower the temperature to 105 degrees and continue dehydrating until the almond pulp is dry (up to 24 hours). Break the pulp into chunks and store in the freezer until you're ready to use it. Before using the almond pulp, grind it into a flour in your blender or food processor.

SOY LECITHIN

Some recipes (desserts, in particular) will call for soy lecithin, which is extracted from soybean oil. This optional ingredient is not Raw. If you use soy lecithin, I highly recommend using a brand that is "non-GMO," meaning it was processed without any genetically modified ingredients (a great brand is Health Alliance®). Soy lecithin helps your dessert (cheesecake, for example) maintain a firmer texture.

17

That said, it's certainly not necessary. If an amount isn't suggested, a good rule of thumb is to use 1 teaspoon per 1 cup total recipe volume.

ICE CREAM FLAVORINGS

When making Raw vegan ice cream, it's better to use alcohol-free extracts so they freeze better.

SWEETENERS

The following is a list of sweeteners that you might see used in my recipes. It's important to know that the healthiest sweeteners are fresh whole fruits, including fresh dates. That said, dates sometimes compromise texture in recipes. As a chef, I look for great texture, and as a health food advocate, I lean towards fresh dates. But as a consultant helping people embrace a Raw vegan lifestyle, I'm also supportive of helping them transition, which sometimes means using raw agave nectar, or some other easy-to-use sweetener that might not have the healthiest ranking in the Raw food world, but is still much healthier than most sweeteners used in the Standard American Diet.

Most of my recipes can use pitted dates in place of raw agave nectar. There is some debate among Raw food enthusiasts as to whether agave nectar is Raw. The company I use (Madhava®) claims to be Raw and says they do not heat their Raw agave nectar above 118 degrees. If however, you still want to eat the healthiest of sweeteners, then bypass the raw agave nectar and use pitted dates. In most recipes, you can simply substitute 1-2 pitted dates for 1 tablespoon of raw agave nectar. Dates won't give you a super creamy texture, but the texture can be improved by making a "date paste" (pureeing pitted and soaked dates - with their soak water, plus some additional water, if necessary - in a food processor fitted with the "S" blade). This, of course, takes a little extra time.

If using raw agave nectar is easier and faster for you, then go ahead and use it; just be sure to buy the Raw version that says they don't heat the agave above 118 degrees (see KristensRaw.com/store for links to this product). And, again, if you're looking to go as far as you can on the spectrum of health, then I recommend using pitted dates. Most of my recipes say raw agave nectar because that is most convenient for people.

Agave Nectar

There are a variety of agave nectars on the market, but again, not all of them are Raw. Make sure it is labeled "Raw" on the bottle *as well as claiming that it isn't processed above 118 degrees*. Just because the label says "Raw" does not necessarily mean it is so... do a double check and make sure it also claims not to be heated above the 118 degrees cut-off. Agave nectar is noteworthy for having a low glycemic index.

Dates

Dates are probably the healthiest of sweeteners, because they're a fresh whole food. Fresh organic dates are filled with nutrition, including calcium and magnesium. I like to call dates, "Nature's Candy."

Feel free to use dates instead of agave or honey in Raw vegan recipes. If a recipe calls for 1/2 cup of raw agave, then you can substitute with approximately 1/2 cup of pitted dates. You can also make your own date sugar by dehydrating pitted dates and then grinding them down. This is a great alternative to Rapadura®.

Honey

Most honey is technically raw, but it is not vegan by most definitions of "vegan" because it is produced by animals, who therefore are at risk of being mistreated. While honey does not have the health risks associated with animal byproducts such as eggs or dairy, it can spike the body's natural sugar levels. Agave nectar has a lower, healthier glycemic index and can replace any recipe you find that calls for honey, in a 1 to 1 ratio.

Maple Syrup

Maple syrup is made from boiled sap of the maple tree. It is not considered Raw, but some people still use it as a sweetener in certain dishes.

Rapadura®

This is a dried sugarcane juice, and it's not Raw. It is, however, an unrefined and unbleached organic whole-cane sugar. It imparts a nice deep sweetness to your recipes, even if you only use a little. Feel free to omit it if you'd like to adhere to a strictly Raw program. You can substitute Rapadura with home-made date sugar (see Dates above).

Stevia

This is from the leaf of the stevia plant. It has a sweet taste and doesn't elevate blood sugar levels. It's very sweet, so you'll want to use much less stevia than you would any other sweetener. My mom actually grows her own stevia. It's a great addition in fresh smoothies, for example, to add some sweetness without the calories. You can use the white powdered or liquid version from the store, but these are not Raw. When possible, the best way to have stevia is grow it yourself.

Yacon Syrup

This sweetener has a low glycemic index, making it very attractive to some people. It has a molasses-type flavor that is nice and rich. You can replace raw agave with this sweetener in my recipes, but make sure to get the Raw variety, available at NaturalZing.com. They offer a few different yacon syrups, including one in particular that is not heat-treated. Be sure to choose that one.

SUN-DRIED TOMATOES

By far, the best sun-dried tomatoes are those you make yourself with a dehydrator. If you don't have a dehydrator, make sure you buy the "dry" sun-dried tomatoes, usually found in the bulk section of your health food market. Don't buy the kind that are packed in a jar of oil.

Also... don't buy sun-dried tomatoes if they're really dark (almost black) because these just don't taste as good. Again, I recommend making them yourself if you truly want the freshest flavor possible. It's really fun to do!

EATING WITH YOUR EYES

Most of us, if not all, naturally eat with our eyes before taking a bite of food. So, do yourself a favor and make your eating experience the best ever with the help of a simple, gorgeous presentation. Think of it this way, with real estate, it's always *location, location, location*, right? Well, with food, it's always *presentation, presentation, presentation.*

Luckily, Raw food does this on its own with all of its naturally vibrant and bright colors. But I take it even one step farther—I use my best dishes when I eat. I use my beautiful wine glasses for my smoothies and juices. I use my fancy goblets for many of my desserts. Why? Because I'm worth it. And, so are you! Don't save your good china just for company. Believe me, you'll notice the difference. Eating well is an attitude, and when you take care of yourself, your body will respond in kind.

ONLINE RESOURCES FOR GREAT PRODUCTS

For a complete and detailed list of my favorite kitchen tools, products, and various foods (all available online), please visit: KristensRaw.com/store.

BOOK RECOMMENDATIONS

I highly recommend reading the following life-changing books.

- *Diet for a New America*, by John Robbins
- *The Food Revolution*, by John Robbins
- *The China Study*, by T. Colin Campbell
- *Skinny Bitch*, by Rory Freedman

MEASUREMENT CONVERSIONS

1 tablespoon = 3 teaspoons

1 ounce = 2 tablespoons

1/4 cup = 4 tablespoons

1/3 cup = 5 1/3 tablespoons

1 cup

= 8 ounces

= 16 tablespoons

= 1/2 pint

1/2 quart

= 1 pint

= 2 cups

1 gallon

= 4 quarts

= 8 pints

= 16 cups

= 128 ounces

BASIC RECIPES TO KNOW

Nourishing Rejuvelac

Yield 1 gallon

Rejuvelac is a cheesy-tasting liquid that is rich in enzymes and healthy flora to support a healthy intestine and digestion.

23

Get comfortable making this super easy recipe because its use goes beyond just drinking it between meals.

1 cup soft wheat berries, rye berries, or a mixture
water

Place the wheat berries in a half-gallon jar and fill the jar with water. Screw the lid on the jar and soak the wheat berries overnight(10 - 12 hours) on your counter. The next morning, drain and rinse them. Sprout the wheat berries for 2 days, draining and rinsing 1 - 2 times a day.

Then, fill the jar with purified water and screw on the lid, or cover with cheesecloth secured with a rubber band. Allow to ferment for 24 - 36 hours, or until the desired tartness is achieved. It should have a cheesy, almost tart/lemony flavor and scent.

Strain your rejuvelac into another glass jar and store in the refrigerator for up to 5 - 7 days. For a second batch using the same sprouted wheat berries, fill the same jar of already sprouted berries with water again, and allow to ferment for 24 hours. Strain off the rejuvelac as you did the time before this. You can do this process yet again, noting that each time the rejuvelac gets a little weaker in flavor.

Enjoy 1/4 - 1 cup of *Nourishing Rejuvelac* first thing in the morning and/or between meals. It's best to start with a small amount and work your way up as your body adjusts.

Suggestion:

- For extra nutrition and incredible flavor, *Nourishing Rejuvelac* can be used in various recipes such as Raw vegan cheeses, desserts, smoothies, soups, dressings and more. Simply use it in place of the water required by the recipe.

Crème Fraiche

Yield approximately 2 cups

> 1 cup cashews, soaked 1 hour, drained, and rinsed
> 1/4 - 1/2 cup *Nourishing Rejuvelac* (see above)
> 1 - 2 tablespoons raw agave nectar

Blend the ingredients until smooth. Store in an airtight glass mason jar for up to 5 days. This freezes well, so feel free to make a double batch for future use.

Nut/Seed Milk (regular)

Yield 4 - 5 cups

The creamiest nut/seed milk traditionally comes from hemp seeds, cashews, pine nuts, Brazil nuts or macadamia nuts, although I'm also a huge fan of milks made from walnuts, pecans, hazelnuts, almonds, sesame seeds, and others.

This recipe does not include a sweetener, but when I'm in the mood for a little sweetness, I add a couple of pitted dates or a squirt of raw agave nectar. Yum!

> 1 1/2 cups nuts, soaked 6 - 12 hours, drained and rinsed
>
> 3 1/4 cups water
>
> pinch Himalayan crystal salt, optional

Blend the ingredients until smooth and deliciously creamy. For an even *extra creamy* texture, strain your nut/seed milk through a nut milk bag.

Sweet Nut/Seed Cream (thick)

Yield 2 - 3 cups

> 1 cup nuts or seeds, soaked 6 - 8 hours, drained and rinsed
>
> 1 - 1 1/2 cups water, more if needed
>
> 2 - 3 tablespoons raw agave nectar or 2 - 3 dates, pitted
>
> 1/2 teaspoon vanilla extract, optional

Blend all of the ingredients until smooth.

Raw Mustard

Yield approximately 1 1/2 - 2 cups

> 1 - 2 tablespoons yellow mustard seeds (depending on how "hot" you want it), soaked 1 - 2 hours
>
> 1 1/2 cups extra virgin olive oil or hemp oil
>
> 1 1/2 tablespoons dry mustard powder
>
> 2 tablespoons apple cider vinegar
>
> 2 tablespoons fresh lemon juice
>
> 3 dates, pitted and soaked 30-minutes, drained
>
> 1/2 cup raw agave nectar
>
> 1 teaspoon Himalayan crystal salt
>
> pinch turmeric

Blend all of the ingredients together until smooth. It might be very thick, so if you want, add some water or oil to help thin it out. Adding more oil will help reduce the "heat" if it's too spicy for your taste.

Variation:

- *Honey Mustard Version:* Add another 1/3 cup raw agave nectar (or more, depending on how sweet you want it)

My Basic Raw Mayonnaise

Yield about 2 1/2 cups

People tell me all the time how much they like this recipe.

1 cup cashews, soaked 1 - 2 hours, drained

1/2 teaspoon paprika

2 cloves garlic

1 teaspoon onion powder

3 tablespoons fresh lemon juice

1/4 cup extra virgin olive oil or hemp oil

2 tablespoons parsley, chopped

2 tablespoons water, if needed

Blend all of the ingredients, except the parsley, until creamy. Pulse in the parsley. My Basic Raw Mayonnaise will stay fresh for up to one week in the refrigerator.

CHAPTER 2

IT'S TIME FOR DESSERT!

Raw vegan desserts are the perfect solution for anyone who loves sweets but wants to avoid refined carbohydrates and sugars, dairy products, and unhealthful fats. Almost any dessert you can make cooked — cookies, pies, cakes, tarts, crisps, ice creams, and candies — you can make Raw vegan! Here's a secret though... your family and friends will never know the difference, since they taste as rich and sweet as their traditional counterparts.

I'm often asked for simple ways to start living a Raw vegan or HRAV (High Raw-All Vegan) lifestyle. Raw vegan desserts are a great starting point. By simply replacing your traditional, artery-clogging, blood sugar spiking desserts with delicious Raw vegan desserts, you (and your family) can easily start your journey to optimal health.

CINNAMON BANANA CANDY

Yield, well... as much as you make ☺

Easy and delicious... it doesn't get much easier than this. (You'll need a dehydrator.)

1 - 5 bananas, peeled, sliced lengthwise

1 tablespoon cinnamon, more or less depending on the number of slices you make

Place the sliced bananas on a mesh dehydrator sheet. Sprinkle them lightly with the cinnamon (or heavily, depending on how much you like cinnamon). Dehydrate these delicious treats at 140 degrees for approximately 45 minutes, then lower the temperature to 105 degrees and dehydrate until desired texture (anywhere from 6 - 20 hours).

SIMPLE BANANA SMASH PUDDING

Yield 2 servings

Kids love to make this! Even though this is a satiating dessert, it also makes a terrific breakfast (you'll find this is true with most Raw vegan desserts – yippee!).

  2 bananas, peeled and chopped

  1/4 cup raw nuts/seeds of your choice (I love hemp seeds)

  1/4 cup dried fruit of your choice (goji berries, raisins or currants are perfect)

  dash cinnamon

  dash nutmeg

Smash the bananas in a bowl with a fork and stir in the nuts, dried fruit, cinnamon, and nutmeg. Voila, you're done! Serve immediately.

BANANAS FOSTER

See color photo at KristensRaw.com/photos.

Yield 2 servings

This is so amazing! Oh my... I'll write it again... this is so amazing! Even if you only make the glaze and drizzle it on plain bananas. This is to live for!!!

The Main Components

1 cup *Raw Vanilla Ice Cream* (see recipe in the ice cream section)

2 bananas, peeled and sliced

2 tablespoons chopped walnuts

The Glaze

1/4 cup raw agave nectar

1 tablespoon raw carob powder

2 teaspoons extra virgin olive oil or hemp oil

1/4 teaspoon rum extract

dash vanilla extract

pinch cinnamon

Blend all of the ingredients together for the glaze. Drizzle over the sliced bananas, walnuts and Raw vanilla ice cream.

CRANBERRY CANDY

Yield 15 - 20 candy balls

These are really delicious. It's almost impossible to eat just one. And, they're so easy to make that you have to try them right away.

2 cups raw macadamia nuts

1/3 cup dried coconut, shredded & unsweetened

pinch Himalayan crystal salt

2 cups dried cranberries

3/4 cup raisins

Process the macadamia nuts, coconut and salt in a food processor, fitted with the "S" blade, until coarsely ground. Add the dried cranberries and raisins and continue processing until the mixture begins to stick together when pressed between your fingers. Roll into balls of desired size. These freeze great.

Variations:

- Use almonds, walnuts, pistachios or pecans in place of the macadamia nuts
- Substitute dried apricots, goji berries, dried cherries, dried pineapple (chopped) or dates (pitted and chopped) in place of the cranberries and/or raisins.

ISLE OF CAPRI CHOCOLATE MOUSSE

Yield 2 - 2 1/2 cups

This delicious, rich and refreshing dessert was inspired by the Isle of Capri, where they grow tons of lemons and use this beautiful citrus in almost all of their food!

1/3 cup fresh lemon juice

2 avocados, pitted and peeled

3/4 cup raw agave nectar

3/4 cup raw chocolate powder or raw carob powder

zest from 1 whole lemon

Blend all of the ingredients until creamy. This freezes beautifully.

PEPPERMINT CHOCOLATE MOUSSE

See color photo at KristensRaw.com/photos.

Yield 2 – 2 1/2 cups

Mint chocolate has always been one of my favorites, ever since I was a kid. I'm so thrilled to have this healthy and awesome replacement to my former favorite, mint chocolate ice cream. It's divinely refreshing, rich and you can't help but close your eyes to relish it with each bite.

> 1/3 cup peppermint-flavored bottled water from Metromint® or plain water
>
> 2 avocados, pitted and peeled
>
> 3/4 cup raw agave nectar or pitted dates, packed
>
> 3/4 cup raw chocolate powder or raw carob powder
>
> 1 teaspoon peppermint extract

Blend all of the ingredients until creamy. It's wonderful to eat right away or chilled in the refrigerator or you can freeze it in a glass mason jar or an ice cube tray for Frozen Peppermint Chocolate Mousse Bites!

SWEET DRAGON PUFF MOUSSE

Yield approximately 3 1/2 cups

Oh my goodness, you have to try this. It's delicious, creamy and fantastically light in your mouth. Forget that it's made with avocado and that it's green (although green is my favorite color, so I love it!), because it's divinely exquisite and gently melts on your tongue. Bonus: this is another one of those perfect recipes for breakfast!

3 avocados, pitted, peeled

1 cup fresh orange juice

3 tablespoons fresh lime juice

2 - 3 tablespoons raw agave nectar (or more to taste!)

1 teaspoon vanilla extract

Put all of the ingredients into a blender and process until you reach a smooth and creamy consistency. This dessert should be eaten immediately for freshness.

SEXED UP SPICY CHOCOLATE MOUSSE

Yield approximately 2 cups

You can't help but feel a little sexy when you're licking Raw Chocolate Mousse off a spoon that is spicy and makes your tongue tingle.

1/4 - 1/2 cup water

2 avocados, pitted and peeled

3/4 cup raw agave nectar

3/4 cup raw chocolate powder or raw carob powder

1 teaspoon vanilla extract

3/4 teaspoon cayenne pepper (or more!)

1/4 teaspoon Himalayan crystal salt

34

Blend all of the ingredients in a blender until smooth and creamy. It's wonderful to eat right away or chilled in the refrigerator or you can freeze it in a glass mason jar or an ice cube tray for Frozen Sexed Up Spicy Chocolate Mousse Bites!

ORANGE BLOSSOM CHOCOLATE MOUSSE

Yield 1 1/4 cup

This is one of my mom's favorite recipes. She loves the flavor of orange blossom! (Fun beauty tip: I love using orange blossom water with a cotton ball on my face after washing it, as a refreshing toner.)

    2 tablespoons water
    2 tablespoons orange blossom water*
    1/4 cup + 2 tablespoons raw agave nectar
    1/4 cup raw chocolate powder
    2 tablespoons raw carob powder
    3/4 teaspoon almond extract
    1 avocado, pitted and peeled

Blend all of the ingredients in your blender until smooth and creamy. It's wonderful to eat right away or chilled in the refrigerator or you can freeze it in a glass mason jar or an ice cube tray for Frozen Orange Blossom Chocolate Bites!

* Orange blossom water can be found at most Middle Eastern Markets, online, and at some Whole Foods Markets.

KEY LIME PUDDING

Yield approximately 1 cup

All of my clients rave on and on about this dessert. If they only knew how simple and easy it is to make.

2 avocados, pitted and peeled

1/2 cup raw agave nectar

1/3 cup fresh lime juice (from key limes, if possible, otherwise regular limes work great)

1 teaspoon fresh lime zest

Blend all of the ingredients until smooth and deliciously creamy. Garnish with lime wedges, if desired. Key Lime Pudding freezes wonderfully so make a double batch and store it for a treat later on.

KEY LIME PERFECT PARFAIT

Yield approximately 4 servings

1 1/2 cups raw macadamia nuts

1/3 cup dried coconut, unsweetened & shredded

pinch Himalayan crystal salt

3/4 cup pitted dates, packed

2 recipes of Key Lime Pudding

Place the nuts, coconut and salt in a food processor, fitted with the "S" blade, and process until you reach a texture that is coarsely ground. Add the dates and process briefly until mixture just begins to stick together. Sprinkle some of the mixture into the bottom of four small cups or wine glasses (reserving enough to layer more in a moment).

Scoop 1/4 cup of the Key Lime Pudding on the top of each nut crumble. Layer a small amount of the nut crumble on top of the Key Lime Pudding. Next is another layer of Key Lime Pudding. Top each dessert with a little nut crumble. Enjoy this delicious creation.

FRUIT – GOURMET STYLE

Yield approximately 1/2 cup of sauce

I like serving this recipe in elegant wine goblets.

The Sauce

3 tablespoons fresh basil, chopped

1/4 cup fresh mint, chopped

1/4 cup raw agave nectar

2 tablespoons fresh lemon juice

1 tablespoon water

Splash of organic vegan white wine, optional

The Fruit

2 cups of blackberries, raspberries, strawberries, blueberries, or any combination of them

Blend all of the ingredients for the sauce and pour over the fruit. Enjoy.

PEACH CARAMEL PIE

Yield one 8 or 9-inch pie

This is really easy to put together and it's mega juicy and delicious. Put peaches on your next shopping list if they're in season, because you need to make this.

The Crust

> 2 cups raw pecans
>
> 2 tablespoons raw carob powder
>
> pinch Himalayan crystal salt
>
> 1 cup raisins

The Pie Filling

> 2/3 cup packed dried apple, ground (see *The Filling*, below)
>
> 1/3 cup soft dates, pitted, chopped
>
> 8 - 10 fresh peaches
>
> 3 tablespoons raw almond butter
>
> 2 tablespoons raw agave nectar
>
> 1/2 teaspoon mesquite meal, optional
>
> 1 teaspoon cinnamon
>
> pinch of nutmeg

The Crust

Grind the pecans, carob and salt in a food processor, fitted with the "S" blade, until coarsely ground. Add the raisins and process until the mixture holds together gently when pressed together between two fingers. Press firmly into an 8 or 9-inch pie pan.

The Filling

Grind the dried apples in a food processor until they're in tiny pieces. Transfer to a large bowl and add the chopped dates. Briefly toss to mix together. Pit and chop the peaches and put approximately 4 cups worth in the bowl with the dried apples and dates. Puree the remaining couple cups of chopped peaches in a blender or food processor with the rest of the ingredients and add to the mixture in the large bowl. Stir well or mix with your hands. Transfer the filling onto the crust. This will stay fresh for up to three days, when stored in a sealed container in the refrigerator.

RICHLY REWARDING CARAMEL APPLE PIE

Yield one 8 or 9-inch pie

The Crust

2 cups raw pecans

pinch Himalayan crystal salt

1 cup raisins

The Filling

2/3 cup packed dried apple, ground (see *The Filling*, below)

1/3 cup soft dates, pitted, chopped

6 fresh apples, cored and shredded (6 cups)

2 - 3 tablespoons raw almond butter

2 tablespoons fresh lemon juice

2 tablespoons raw agave nectar

1/2 teaspoon mesquite meal or lucuma powder, optional

1 teaspoon cinnamon

pinch of nutmeg

The Crust

Grind the pecans and salt in a food processor, fitted with the "S" blade, until coarsely ground. Add the raisins and process until the mixture holds together when gently pressed between two of your fingers. Press the crust mixture firmly into an 8 or 9-inch pie pan.

The Filling

Grind the dried apples in a food processor until they're in tiny pieces. Transfer to a large bowl. Add the chopped dates to the dried apples. Briefly toss to mix.

Gently squeeze out excess juice from the fresh shredded apples before adding them to the dried apples and dates. Combine the fresh apples with the dried apples and dates, along with the almond butter, lemon juice, agave nectar, mesquite meal, cinnamon, and nutmeg. Stir well or mix with your hands. Press the filling into the crust. Store in a sealed container in the refrigerator for up to two days.

CHOCOLATE MINT CHIP PARFAIT

Yield approximately 2 servings

Growing up, my absolute favorite flavor for any dessert was chocolate mint – hands down. So, I had to come up with a creation to satisfy that desire. Here it is. I'm so proud of it because it's perfectly full of chocolate and mint flavor, and so healthy!

The Chocolate Mint Mousse Filling

1/4 cup water

1 avocado, pitted and peeled

1/4 cup + 2 tablespoons raw agave nectar

1/4 cup + 2 tablespoons raw chocolate powder

1/2 teaspoon peppermint extract

1 1/2 tablespoons raw cacao nibs

Blend all of the ingredients, except the cacao nibs, until creamy. Stir in the cacao nibs.

The Chocolate Crumble Mixture

3/4 cup raw pecans, almonds, walnuts, or macadamia nuts (or a mixture)

(continued)

1/2 cup raisins

1 tablespoon raw cacao nibs

1 tablespoon raw chocolate powder

pinch Himalayan crystal salt

Grind the nuts in a food processor, fitted with the "S" blade, until coarsely ground. Add the remaining ingredients and process until the mixture holds together when you pinch it gently between two of your fingers.

The Assembly

Get out some of your fabulous wine glasses. Layer 3 tablespoons of the Chocolate Crumble Mixture into the bottom of each wine glass. Then, follow that with 3 tablespoons of the Chocolate Mint Mousse. Then, again with the Chocolate Crumble Mixture and so on... until you're at the top of your glass or you've used up all of the parfait components.

SINFUL CHERRY ENGLISH TRIFLE

Yield one 8 x 8 baking dish

Don't let the steps in this gourmet dish intimidate you. They each take only minutes to prepare, and it's well worth it!

The Crumble

2 cups raw pecans

(continued)

42

1/8 teaspoon Himalayan crystal salt

1 tablespoon extra virgin coconut oil

1/2 cup dried (bing) cherries

The Cheese Filling

2 cups cashews (soaked 1 - 2 hours), drained & rinsed

1/2 - 3/4 cup *Nourishing Rejuvelac* (see recipe in Ch.1)

1 teaspoon vanilla extract

2 tablespoons raw agave nectar

1 tablespoon fresh lemon zest

1 tablespoon fresh orange zest

The Cherry Filling

2 pounds fresh cherries, pitted or two 12-ounce packages of frozen dark sweet pitted cherries, (about 3 cups), thawed

3/4 cup dates, pitted and soaked 30 minutes, drained

2 tablespoons fresh lemon juice

1 tablespoon raw agave nectar

1 teaspoon orange flavored extract

The Crumble

Process the nuts and salt until coarsely ground in a food processor, fitted with an "S" blade. Add the coconut oil and dried cherries and process until mixture begins to stick together. Firmly, but gently, press 2/3 of the mixture into the bottom of a glass baking dish.

The Cheese Filling

Blend all of the ingredients until creamy. Don't get it too thin (you want a pretty thick consistency). Spread the cheese on top of crumble.

The Cherry Filling

Take 1/3 of the cherries and blend with the dates, lemon juice, agave nectar and orange extract. Add this to the remaining 2/3 of cherries and stir. Layer on top of cheese.

Sprinkle remaining 1/3 of crumble on top of cherries. Refrigerate until ready to serve.

FRESH LEMON PUDDING

Yield approximately 1 cup

This pudding is so refreshing and sweet on a warm spring day (or any time of year!). It reminds me of pure sunshine.

2/3 cup fresh coconut meat from a young Thai coconut

1/3 cup raw agave nectar

1/4 cup fresh lemon juice

1 teaspoon fresh lemon zest

Blend all of ingredients until deliciously smooth and creamy. Garnish with lemon wedges, if desired. This freezes very well.

SUMMER STRAWBERRY COBBLER

See color photo at KristensRaw.com/photos.

Yield one 8 x 8 glass baking dish

I am a fool for Raw vegan cobblers because they're satiating, super easy to prepare, and nutritious. Here's a fun, delicious recipe for exactly that. It's refreshing with flavors that keep playing in your mouth, well after you've swallowed a bite.

The Crumble

2 cups raw pecans or walnuts

3/4 cup dried coconut, shredded & unsweetened

1 teaspoon fresh orange zest

1/2 teaspoon cinnamon

1/4 teaspoon Himalayan crystal salt

2/3 cup currants

1/3 cup prunes, chopped

The Strawberry Filling

25 oz fresh strawberries, destemmed (or use frozen and thaw them)

1/3 cup fresh orange juice

8 soft dates, pitted

2 tablespoons raw agave nectar

The Crumble

Place the nuts, coconut, orange zest, cinnamon, and salt in a food processor, fitted with the "S" blade, and process until coarsely ground. Add the currants and prunes, and process until the mixture resembles coarse crumbs and holds together when gently pressed between two fingers. Set aside.

The Filling

Take about 15 - 16 ounces (approximately two-thirds) of the strawberries, chop them and set aside in a large bowl. Then, place the rest of the strawberries along with the orange juice, dates, and agave in a blender and process until smooth. Pour the blended mixture into the bowl with the chopped strawberries and stir.

The Assembly

Pour half of the crumble in the bottom of the glass baking dish and give it a firm but gentle press. Spread the strawberry filling on top. Sprinkle the remaining cobbler crumble on top of the strawberry filling, allowing some of the beautiful strawberry filling to show through. Serve at room temperature, or warm in a dehydrator for up to an hour at 130 degrees for extra deliciousness. Covered, Summer Strawberry Cobbler will keep for up to three days in the refrigerator.

Serving suggestions and variations:

- Serve with Raw ice cream... recipes later in this book
- Prepare and serve in individual wine glasses or bowls instead of the glass baking dish. Gorgeous!

46

INSANELY GOOD FIESTA COBBLER

Yield one 8 x 13 glass baking dish

Get ready to "WOW" everyone with this party size dessert dish. The colors are fun and beautiful. You'll be very proud to serve this.

The Crumble

3 1/2 cups raw pecan and walnut mixture

1 cup dried coconut, shredded & unsweetened

1/2 teaspoon allspice

1/4 teaspoon Himalayan crystal salt

1 1/2 cups raisins

The Filling #1: Mango

3 bags frozen mango or peaches, thawed

3/4 cup dried mango, soaked and drained (reserve 1/3 cup soak water)

3 tablespoons raw agave nectar

1 tablespoon fresh lime juice

The Filling #2: Raspberry

2 bags frozen raspberries, thawed

(continued)

8 dates pitted, soaked and drained (reserve 1/4 cup soak water)

3 tablespoons raw agave nectar

2 teaspoons fresh lime juice

The Crumble

Using a food processor, fitted with the "S" blade, process the nuts, coconut, allspice and salt until coarsely ground. Add the raisins and process until the mixture begins to stick together when gently pressed between two of your fingers.

Note: You may have to divide in half and do in two batches depending on the size of your food processor.

The Filling #1

Open and pour one bag of the thawed mango into a large bowl (chop any chunks that are too big into bite-size chunks). Blend the other two bags of the thawed mango along with the soaked and drained dried mango, the reserved soak water, agave and lime juice. Pour the blended mango into the bowl with the chunks and stir to mix. Set this mixture aside.

The Filling #2

Open and pour one bag of the thawed raspberries into a medium bowl. Blend the other bag of thawed raspberries along with the soaked and drained dates, the reserved soak water, agave and lime juice. Pour the blended raspberries into the bowl with the whole raspberries and stir to mix.

The Assembly

Pour half of the crumble in the bottom of the glass baking dish and give it a firm but gentle press. Pour alternating rows lengthwise of filling (3 total: yellow on the outside then red in the middle then yellow on the outside again). *NOT one on top of the other, there is only one layer of fruit.* You will probably have some mango filling leftover as well as some raspberry. That's great if you do. *Put them in a mason jar and enjoy in a smoothie later or the next day.* Sprinkle the remaining crumble on top, keeping a little of the fruit color showing through. Refrigerate for up to an hour or more to set. Store covered in the refrigerator for up to three days.

Serving suggestion:

- Serve with Raw ice cream... recipes later in this book

CINNAMON PEACH COBBLER

Yield one 8 x 8 glass baking dish

This is one of my family's favorite recipes!

The Crumble

2 cups raw pecans or walnuts

3/4 cup dried coconut, shredded & unsweetened

1/2 teaspoon cinnamon

1/2 teaspoon ginger powder

(continued)

1/4 teaspoon nutmeg

1/4 teaspoon Himalayan crystal salt

1 cup raisins

The Peach Filling

3 (10-oz) packages frozen peaches, thawed

8 dates, pitted and soaked 30 minutes, drained

3 tablespoons raw agave nectar

3/4 teaspoon cinnamon

The Crumble

Place the nuts, coconut, cinnamon, ginger, nutmeg, and salt in a food processor fitted with the S-blade and process until coarsely ground. Add the raisins and process until the mixture resembles coarse crumbs and begins to stick together.

The Filling

Take 2 packages of the thawed peaches, roughly chop them, and place into a large bowl. Then, place the third package of peaches along with the dates, agave, and cinnamon in a blender and process until smooth. Transfer the blended mixture to the bowl with chopped peaches and stir to mix.

The Assembly

Pour half of the crumble in the bottom of the glass baking dish and give it a firm but gentle press. Spread the peach filling on top. Sprinkle the remaining cobbler topping on top of the peaches, allowing some of the pretty filling to show through. Serve at room temperature, or warm in a dehydrator for extra deliciousness. Cinnamon Peach Cobbler will keep for three days, when stored in the refrigerator.

Green Smoothie & Fruit Popsicles

See color photo at KristensRaw.com/photos.

During the hot summer months, I'm eager to stay "cool" and these Green Smoothie & Fruit Popsicles are the perfect answer. And, kids LOVE them! Say goodbye to unhealthy, artificially flavored supermarket popsicles forever.

By now, most of you are probably experts at making Green Smoothies. If so, then simply freeze your next batch in Popsicle molds. If you're not familiar with Green Smoothies, then check out my blog for details (search: "green smoothies").

Note: when making the recipes below, use a fruit to greens ratio of about 60 - 70% fruit to 30 - 40% greens.

Cinna-Spinach Man

> water
> splash lemon juice
> spinach
> mango
> cinnamon

Blueberry Ginger Affair

water

spinach

splash lemon juice

blueberries

ginger

Pink Princess

Watermelon

Simply blend the ingredients together for the recipe you choose and pour into popsicle molds and freeze. If you don't have popsicle molds, then you can freeze the blended ingredients in an ice cube tray and have Green Smoothie Frozen Bites.

SMILING GIRL FROZEN FUDGIES

Yield 1 cup

Another perfect summertime treat. Ahhh, who am I kidding? These are perfect ANYTIME!

1/2 cup water

1/3 cup raw agave nectar

1 avocado, pitted and peeled

1/3 cup raw chocolate powder

(continued)

1 tablespoon coconut butter

1 tablespoon coconut oil

1 tablespoon hemp protein powder

1/4 teaspoon almond extract (optional)

Blend all of the ingredients until smooth and pour into popsicle molds (or an ice cube tray for Smiling Girl Frozen Fudgie Bites) and freeze. Enjoy with a smile!

FROZEN GRAPES

Yield, well… as many as you freeze ☺

This refreshing dessert is a "must have" in your freezer because they're perfect for popping into your mouth when you need something to "take the sugar edge off."

1 bunch grapes, de-stemmed

Wash the grapes and lightly dry with a paper towel. Put them in a baggie or glass mason jar (preferably) and freeze.

KRISTEN SUZANNE'S FAMOUS HEAVENLY COOKIES

Yield approximately 10 cookie balls

These cookies will be all the rage with your family and friends. They're super easy to make (no equipment needed!) so you'll want to make extras. Trust me!

1/4 cup + 2 tablespoons raw nut butter (almond, pecan, or walnut)

1/2 cup + 2 tablespoons dried coconut, shredded and unsweetened

1/2 cup raisins

2 tablespoons raw agave nectar

1/4 teaspoon vanilla extract

pinch Himalayan crystal salt

dash cinnamon

Stir everything together in a bowl with a spoon (large bowl and spoon if you're making a double or triple batch). Then, take a moment and mash it together with your hands. Yes, it's sticky and gooey, but it's fun and you still have to roll them so you'll be getting sticky and gooey anyway. Using a 1-tablespoon measured amount of cookie batter, roll them into balls. Store these in the refrigerator or freezer.

Variations:

- Stir in 1 tablespoon of raw chocolate powder or raw carob powder
- Roll them in dried, unsweetened coconut or ground nuts

CARNIVAL CARAMEL APPLE

Yield 1 serving

This could very well blow your mind. The dessert is so easy, and when you eat it, you'll swear it tastes just like a caramel apple... just like you used to get at the carnival as a kid!

54

1 large apple (any flavor), cored and chopped

2 tablespoons raw almond butter

2 dates, pitted

Blend all of the ingredients together on low speed for a chunky delicious mixture or at a higher speed for a more apple-saucy texture.

GOURMET RAW GEORGIA STUFFED PEACHES

Yield 4 servings

3/4 cup raw pecans

3 tablespoons dried coconut, shredded & unsweetened

1/4 cup raisins

4 peaches, cut in half and pitted

1 tablespoon Rapadura®

Place the nuts and coconut in a food processor, fitted with the "S" blade, and process until coarsely ground. Add the raisins and process until the mixture starts to stick together. Scoop one tablespoon of the mixture into the hole of each peach half. Sprinkle the top of each dessert lightly with a little Rapadura® and any of the remaining nut mixture. Serve immediately.

FUN CHOCOLATE APPLESAUCE

Yield approximately 1 3/4 cups

Here's a terrifically healthy and fun dessert for anyone wanting something a little lighter, but still fully rich on flavor.

2 apples, cored and chopped

3 dates, pitted

2 tablespoons raw chocolate powder or raw carob powder

3 tablespoons raw almond butter or hemp seed butter

1/4 teaspoon cinnamon

Puree all of the ingredients in a food processor until you reach your desired texture (I like mine a little on the chunky side). Enjoy!

SIMPLE CHEESECAKE CRUST

Yield one 8 or 9-inch cheesecake crust

This basic crust can be used for any flavor of cheesecake. You'll notice some more "gourmet" cheesecake crusts in the recipes throughout, but you can always just make this one for any flavor of cheesecake. They're all simple, but this is the easiest.

2 1/4 cups of any raw nuts or combination of nuts

pinch Himalayan crystal salt

1/2 cup of any dried fruit (raisins or dates work great!)

Use a food processor, fitted with the "S" blade, and grind the nuts with the salt until coarsely ground. Add the dried fruit and process until the mixture begins to stick together when pressed gently between two of your fingers. Press the mixture firmly into an 8 or 9-inch spring form pan. Place in the freezer while you make the filling.

OH MY! IT'S VANILLA CHEESECAKE

Yield one 8 or 9-inch cheesecake

This cheesecake recipe calls for the use of *Nourishing Rejuvelac* (see Chapter 1) because it helps impart a cheesier flavor, typically found in regular cheesecake. You can use plain water, but it's definitely worth making with the rejuvelac for the most exquisite cheesecake experience.

The Crust

2 cups raw walnuts

1/4 cup raw pecans

2 tablespoons dried coconut, shredded & unsweetened

1 tablespoon raw cacao nibs

pinch Himalayan crystal salt

1/2 heaping cup raisins or any dried fruit

The Filling

3 cups cashews, soaked 1 hour, drained and rinsed

3/4 cup raw agave nectar

1/2 cup fresh lemon juice

1/4 cup *Nourishing Rejuvelac*, or water

(continued)

2 tablespoons vanilla extract

pinch Himalayan crystal salt

3/4 cup extra virgin coconut oil

2 tablespoons soy lecithin, optional

The Crust

Use a food processor, fitted with the "S" blade, and grind the nuts, coconut, cacao nibs and salt until coarsely ground. Add the dried fruit and process until the mixture begins to gently stick together when pressed between two of your fingers. Press the crust mixture firmly into an 8 or 9-inch spring form pan. Place in the freezer while you make the filling.

The Filling

Blend all of the ingredients, except coconut oil and soy lecithin, in a food processor until creamy (5 - 7 minutes). You may need to stop every couple of minutes to scrape down the sides.

Add the coconut oil and process to incorporate well. Add the soy lecithin and briefly process to incorporate. Pour the filling on top of the crust and smooth the top of it with an offset spatula.

You can freeze the cheesecake for a couple of hours or overnight. Then, let it thaw in your refrigerator (or on top of your counter) for at least an hour before serving. Oh My! It's Vanilla Cheesecake will stay fresh for up to a week, when stored in an airtight container, in your refrigerator. Or, freeze it for up to six months.

RASPBERRY VANILLA CHEESECAKE

See color photo at KristensRaw.com/photos.

Yield one 8 or 9-inch cheesecake

This is one of my most requested recipes. This cheesecake not only tastes delightful, but its vibrant color adds beauty to any dinner table.

The Crust

2 cups raw pecans

1/4 cup hemp seeds

pinch Himalayan crystal salt

1/2 cup raisins (or any dried fruit)

The Filling

3 cups cashews, soaked 1 hour, drained and rinsed

1 cup fresh raspberries

3/4 cup raw agave nectar

1/2 cup fresh lemon juice

2 tablespoons vanilla extract

pinch Himalayan crystal salt

3/4 cup extra virgin coconut oil

2 tablespoons soy lecithin, optional

The Crust

Use a food processor, fitted with the "S" blade, and grind the nuts, seeds, and salt until coarsely ground. Add the raisins and process until the mixture begins to gently stick together when pressed between two of your fingers. Press the crust mixture firmly into an 8 or 9-inch spring form pan. Place in the freezer while you make the filling.

The Filling

Blend all of the ingredients, except coconut oil and soy lecithin, in a food processor until creamy (5 - 7 minutes). You may need to stop every couple of minutes to scrape down the sides.

Add the coconut oil and process to incorporate well. Add the soy lecithin and briefly process to incorporate. Pour the filling on top of the crust and smooth the top of it with an offset spatula.

You can freeze the cheesecake for a couple of hours or overnight. Then, let it thaw in your refrigerator (or on top of your counter) for at least an hour before serving. Raspberry Vanilla Cheesecake will stay fresh for up to a week, when stored in an airtight container, in your refrigerator. Or, freeze it for up to six months.

SUMMER FRESH LEMON CHEESECAKE

See color photo on the cover.

Yield one 8 or 9-inch cheesecake

Refreshing, vibrant, gorgeous, and heavenly! This is one of my favorite Raw vegan desserts to make, especially when I'm bringing a dessert to show off at someone else's house or for a party.

The Crust

3/4 cup dried coconut, shredded and unsweetened

zest of 1 lemon

pinch Himalayan crystal salt

1 3/4 cups hemp seeds

3/4 cup golden raisins

The Filling

3 cups cashews, soaked 1 hour, drained and rinsed

3/4 cup fresh lemon juice

3/4 cup raw (light) agave nectar

1 1/2 tablespoons lemon extract

1 teaspoon turmeric

pinch Himalayan crystal salt

3/4 cup extra virgin coconut oil

2 tablespoons soy lecithin, optional

The Crust

Using a food processor, fitted with the "S" blade, grind the coconut until it's more like a coarse powder. Add the lemon zest, salt, and hemp seeds and process briefly to thoroughly mix the ingredients. Add the raisins and process until the mixture begins to stick together if gently pressed between two of your fingers. Press the crust mixture firmly into an 8 or 9-inch spring form pan. Place in the freezer while you make the filling.

The Filling

Blend all of the ingredients together, except the coconut oil and soy lecithin, until smooth. This could take 5 - 7 minutes, and you might need to stop every couple of minutes to scrape down the sides of the food processor and make sure it's not getting too warm.

Add the coconut oil and process until well incorporated. Add the soy lecithin and process briefly to mix. Pour the mixture on top of the crust in your spring form pan. You can freeze the cheesecake for a couple of hours or overnight. Then, let it thaw in your refrigerator (or on top of your counter) for at least an hour before serving. Summer Fresh Lemon Cheesecake will stay fresh for up to a week, when stored in an airtight container, in your refrigerator. Or, freeze it for up to six months.

DECADENT CHOCOLATE HAZELNUT CHEESECAKE

Yield one 8 or 9-inch cheesecake

The Crust

1 1/2 cups raw hazelnuts
3/4 cup raw walnuts

(continued)

1/8 teaspoon Himalayan crystal salt

2 teaspoons raw chocolate powder

2/3 cup raisins

1/4 teaspoon hazelnut extract

The Filling

3 cups cashews, soaked 1 hour, drained and rinsed

1/3 cup raw agave nectar

1/3 cup soft dates, pitted and packed

1/2 cup fresh lemon juice

1/4 cup water

2 teaspoons hazelnut extract

1 cup extra virgin coconut oil

3/4 cup raw chocolate powder or raw carob powder

2 tablespoons soy lecithin, optional

The Crust

Place the nuts and salt in a food processor, fitted with the "S" blade, and process until coarsely ground. Add the chocolate powder and process briefly. Add the raisins and hazelnut extract and process briefly until the mixture begins to stick together when gently pressed between two of your fingers. Press firmly into the bottom of an 8 or 9-inch spring form pan. Place in the freezer while you make the filling.

The Filling

Blend the cashews, agave nectar, dates, lemon juice, water, and hazelnut extract until creamy. This could last 5 - 7 minutes. Stop every couple of minutes to make sure it's not too hot.

Add the coconut oil and raw chocolate and process until mixed thoroughly. Add the soy lecithin and process briefly to incorporate. Pour the mixture on top of the crust in your spring form pan. You can freeze the cheesecake for a couple of hours or overnight. Then, let it thaw in your refrigerator (or on top of your counter) for at least an hour before serving. Decadent Chocolate Hazelnut Cheesecake will stay fresh for up to a week, when stored in an airtight container, in your refrigerator. Or, freeze it for up to six months.

SWEETLY SOUTHERN VANILLA PEACHES

Yield 4 servings

6 - 7 ripe peaches, pitted and chopped

1/2 cup raw agave nectar

1/3 cup young Thai coconut water

1/2 cup young Thai coconut meat

1 whole vanilla bean, split in half lengthwise, seeds scraped

1/2 fresh lemon, zested

1/4 teaspoon vanilla extract

2 teaspoons fresh lemon juice

2 tablespoons dried coconut, shredded & unsweetened

Place the chopped peaches into a bowl. Blend the agave nectar, coconut water, coconut meat, vanilla bean seeds, lemon zest, vanilla extract, and lemon juice until smooth. Transfer this mixture to the chopped peaches and stir to mix.

Scoop peaches and sauce into four serving bowls and top with the shredded coconut.

SWANKY SEED-N-NUT BALLS

Yield about 10 balls

    1/4 cup raw pumpkin seeds
    1/4 cup raw (hulled) sesame seeds
    15 raw almonds*
    1/4 cup raw walnuts*
    2 tablespoons raw tahini
    3 tablespoons raw agave nectar
    1 tablespoon raw almond butter (or any raw nut butter)
    1/4 cup dried coconut, shredded & unsweetened

In a food processor, fitted with an "S" blade, grind the pumpkin seeds, sesame seeds, almonds, and walnuts together until coarsely ground. Add the tahini, agave nectar and almond butter; and process together well. Using a tablespoon, form the mixture into balls and roll in the coconut. Refrigerate or freeze.

* Use any kind of nut that you have on hand.

PINEAPPLE STRAWBERRY ECSTASY

Yield 4 - 6 servings

    1 (small) fresh, pineapple, peeled, cored and chopped

(continued)

1/2 cup strawberries, destemmed and chopped

1/2 cup dried coconut, shredded & unsweetened

1/4 cup raw agave nectar

1/2 teaspoon rum extract

Place the fruit and coconut into a bowl and toss to mix. Stir the rum extract into the agave, pour over the fruit mixture, and gently toss to mix. Serve at room temperature or chilled.

VANILLA CARIBBEAN PUDDING

Yield 3 cups

This creamy pudding is filled with such healthy and nutritious ingredients that I've been known to eat it as both a breakfast and a dessert dish! Why not?

1 banana, peeled

1 1/2 cups mango, peeled, pitted and chopped (or use frozen mango)

1/2 cup meat from young Thai coconut

1/2 cup water from young Thai coconut

6 dates, pitted, soaked 15 minutes, drained

1/2 vanilla bean, chopped

1/4 teaspoon allspice

1/8 teaspoon cinnamon

2 teaspoons psyllium powder, optional

Blend all of the ingredients together, except the psyllium powder, until creamy. Pulse in the psyllium powder (if desired) and let set for a few minutes before serving. Or, leave out the psyllium powder and chill the pudding for 20-30 minutes prior to serving.

OATMEAL DATE MAPLE COOKIES

Yield 3 cups cookie dough (20 - 24 cookies)

These are a great alternative to the unhealthy after-school snack that kids typically eat... and remember to take some out for yourself, too!

3/4 cup raw oats (available at NaturalZing.com)

3/4 cup raw pecans

3/4 cup raw walnuts

10 soft dates, pitted

1/2 cup golden raisins

3/4 teaspoon maple extract (see FrontierCoop.com)

1/2 teaspoon cinnamon

1/8 teaspoon Himalayan crystal salt

1/8 teaspoon nutmeg

Grind the oats in a food processor, fitted with the "S" blade, until ground. Transfer the ground oats to a bowl. Grind the nuts in the food processor until coarsely ground. Add the oats back to the food processor and briefly mix with the nuts to incorporate.

Add the remaining ingredients and process until it begins to stick together, almost like a cookie dough. Take about 2 tablespoons worth and roll the dough into balls and then flatten into the shape of cookies.

For extra deliciousness, warm these in the dehydrator at 110 - 115 degrees for up to an hour or so before serving. Oh my goodness… they are divine! Store Oatmeal Date Maple Cookies in an airtight container in the refrigerator for up to 2-weeks or in the freezer for up to six months.

"I MUST BE IN HAWAII" DESSERT

Yield 2 servings

If you're going to Hawaii, then this is a great prelude. If you're not going, that's ok, too. Make this fabulous dessert, put on your straw hat and sunglasses, and "act as if."

- 1 cup fresh pineapple, chopped
- 1 banana, peeled and sliced
- 1/4 cup raw agave nectar
- zest of 2 limes
- 1/4 cup of fresh lime juice
- 1 teaspoon fresh ginger, peeled and grated
- 2 tablespoons dried coconut, shredded & unsweetened

Place the fruit on two plates (if I was serving this to you at my house, I'd use my best wine goblets or glasses – just something to consider). Combine the remaining ingredients, except the coconut, and drizzle over the fruit. Sprinkle the coconut on top.

OUT OF THIS GALAXY CHOCOLATE BROWNIES

Yield 12 brownies

Story has it when I was in second grade I threw my lunch box at the bus driver. He must have said something to upset me. If mom had packed these, I wouldn't have thrown it no matter how mad I got.

2 cups raw pecans

3/4 cup raw macadamia nuts

pinch Himalayan crystal salt

1/4 teaspoon cinnamon

1/2 cup raw chocolate powder or raw carob powder

2 tablespoons raw agave nectar

1/2 teaspoon vanilla extract

2 tablespoons dried coconut, shredded & unsweetened

1 cup soft dates, pitted and packed

Grind the nuts, salt, and cinnamon in a food processor, fitted with the "S" blade, until they are coarsely ground. Add the raw chocolate, agave nectar, vanilla, and coconut and process briefly to incorporate. Add the dates and continue processing until the mixture starts to stick together. Press into an 8 x 8 glass baking dish and enjoy. These brownies freeze wonderfully, too!

Variations:

- Roll these into cookie balls
- Swap out the dates for raisins or dried cherries
- Use a variety of raw nuts such as almonds, walnuts, pecans, or hazelnuts

ORANGE BLOSSOM SWEET STUFFING

Yield 1 cup

I made this recipe for one of my clients and he loved it. In fact, his response was, "I could eat this every day." It's one of my all-time favorites, too.

1 1/2 cups raw walnuts or pecans

1/4 cup Rapadura® or date sugar*

2 tablespoons orange blossom water**

1 teaspoon ground cardamom

Grind the nuts in a food processor, fitted with the "S" blade until coarsely ground. Add the Rapadura, orange blossom water and cardamom and pulse to mix.

* You can make date sugar by dehydrating dates and grinding them into a sugar or buy it online.

** You can find this at most Middle Eastern markets, online, and at some Whole Food Markets.

Serving suggestions:

- Eat right out of the bowl with a spoon ☺
- Enjoy on top of ice cream
- Roll into sticky balls
- Eat with your favorite fruit
- Stuff an orange or yellow bell pepper with it and make yourself a lunch worthy of envy.
- Sprinkle on top of a salad. Amazing!

UNIVERSITY OF MICHIGAN BLUEBERRY BANANA PIE

Yield one 8-inch pie

I had to name something after my alma mater, University of Michigan, so this was perfect with the "blue" berries and "yellow" bananas. What's even better is that it literally takes about 10 minutes to make.

4 cups fresh blueberries, washed and drained

1 cup soft dates, pitted & chopped

1 cup raw pecans

1 cup raisins

2 ripe bananas, peeled and sliced

Place the blueberries and dates in a blender and blend together. Next, grind the pecans in a food processor, fitted with the "S" blade, until coarsely ground. Add the raisins and process until the mixture sticks together when gently pressed between two fingers. Firmly press the nut and raisin mixture (this is your pie crust), into an 8-inch glass baking dish. Layer the banana slices on top of the crust and pour the blueberry filling on top of the bananas. Refrigerate for at least three hours and serve as pie.

Variations:

- Use any kind of berries for this easy pie, just remember to change the name ☺
- Use any kind of nuts or seeds and any variety of dried fruit for the crust

THE CRAZY GOOD BAR

Yield one 8 x 8 glass baking dish

Oh my gosh... these are so lip smacking and crazy good! They're one of those EASY desserts that you can store in the freezer and have on hand whenever your sweet tooth emerges. (Remember: this is the kind of thing that makes the Raw vegan lifestyle extra easy. I highly encourage you to have a ready-to-eat supply in your freezer.)

> 2 cups raw walnuts
>
> 2 tablespoons raw chocolate powder or raw carob powder
>
> 1 tablespoon Rapadura®, optional
>
> 1/2 teaspoon almond extract
>
> pinch cinnamon
>
> 1 cup soft dates, pitted
>
> 1/2 cup raisins
>
> 1/4 cup dried cranberries

Grind the walnuts in a food processor fitted with the "S" blade until coarsely ground. Add the delicious raw chocolate powder, Rapadura, almond extract and cinnamon and pulse to mix. Add the dates, raisins and dried cranberries and process until mixture sticks together when pressed between two of your fingers. Press the super yummy mixture firmly into a glass baking dish. Cut these crazy good treats into squares and enjoy. Refrigerate or freeze.

SESAME SEED CANDY

Yield approximately 15 candies

Do you ever get up around 2:00am because you can't sleep? Try munching on these in your jammies. Hopefully you can find a great old black and white movie to watch, too.

1 cup raw (hulled) sesame seeds

1/4 teaspoon cinnamon

pinch nutmeg

2 tablespoons raw agave nectar, or more to taste

1/4 teaspoon almond extract

1/4 cup raisins

1/4 cup Turkish dried apricots, chopped

Place the sesame seeds, cinnamon and nutmeg in a food processor, fitted with the "S" blade, and process the mixture until it's a fine grind. Then, add the agave nectar and almond extract and continue processing until it is smooth. Pulse in the raisins and Turkish dried apricots. Use a tablespoon to shape small amounts into flat rounds or roll into balls.

CHAPTER 3

THE BEST ICE CREAM, HANDS DOWN!

You don't need to have an ice cream maker to make any of these delicious and creamy Raw vegan ice creams. It can make it more fun though, especially if you have kids, making this a great way to involve kids in eating Raw. Just pour any of the following recipes into an ice cream maker and freeze according to the manufacturer's directions.

Note: the directions for the following ice cream recipes will direct you to just "freeze" the recipe. Obviously, if you have a cool ice cream maker, then by all means... use it. ☺ If you don't have an ice cream maker, then you can freeze the ice cream in a shallow 8 x 8 glass baking dish covered with saran wrap.

Another alternative: I sometimes like to freeze my ice cream in small (1-cup), individual glass mason jars. Then, when I want to enjoy some, I can simply take out a jar at a time, and not have to thaw a larger portion just to eat one serving and then re-freeze the remaining portion. This helps keep the ice cream fresh.

When you're ready to eat your Raw vegan ice cream, you'll probably want to take it out of the freezer approximately 10 - 15 minutes prior to serving to thaw. It's also important to note that when using extracts to flavor ice creams, get the alcohol free version because this facilitates freezing.

SUMMER STRAWBERRY ICE CREAM

Yield 3 - 4 servings

I know someone with a pet monkey, and this is the monkey's favorite dessert! That is quite an endorsement if you ask me. ☺

1/2 pound fresh strawberries, stems taken off

1 cup cashews, soaked 1 - 2 hours, drained and rinsed

1/2 cup pitted dates, packed, (soaked 30 minutes, drained) and chopped

1/2 cup water, if needed

Blend all of the ingredients until smooth and creamy, adding some water, if needed. Freeze.

VANILLA ROSE ICE CREAM

Yield 4 - 5 servings

Did you know the vanilla pod comes from the Vanilla Planifolia Orchid? It's the only orchid of 20,000 orchid varieties that bears anything edible. Pretty cool, eh?

1 cup cashews, soaked 1 - 2 hours, drained and rinsed

1/4 - 1 cup young Thai coconut water, as needed*

meat from 1 young Thai coconut

2/3 cup raw agave nectar

2 teaspoons vanilla extract, alcohol free

1 tablespoon rose water**

Blend all of the ingredients in your blender until deliciously smooth and creamy, adding the necessary amount of coconut water to keep it blending for a nice thick texture.

* Start with the lesser amount of coconut water and add more as needed. Freeze.

** You can find rose water at most Middle Eastern stores, online, and at some Whole Foods Markets.

RAW VANILLA BEAN ICE CREAM

Yield 4 servings

    1 cup cashews, unsoaked
    1 whole vanilla bean, ground
    1/2 - 3/4 cup young Thai coconut water*
    meat from 1 young Thai coconut
    1/2 cup raw agave nectar

Grind the nuts in your food processor, fitted with the "S" blade, until coarsely ground. Grind the vanilla bean in a coffee grinder. Place the ground cashews and vanilla bean with the remaining ingredients in a blender and blend until nice and creamy.

* Start with the lesser amount of coconut water and add more as needed. Freeze.

AWESOMELY RICH CHOCOLATE ALMOND ICE CREAM

Yield 4 - 5 servings

I love the richness of this dessert. It's sure to fix any chocolate craving you have.

  2 cups cashews, soaked 1- 2 hours, drained and rinsed

  1/2 cup raw chocolate powder or raw carob powder

  1/2 cup raw yacon syrup or dark (amber) agave*

  1/2 cup young Thai coconut meat

  1/4 - 1/2 cup young Thai coconut water**

  1 banana, peeled and chopped

  1/2 cup raw almonds, chopped

Blend all of the ingredients, except the chopped almonds, in a blender until smooth and creamy, adding enough of the coconut water to keep it blending (but still keeping it nice and thick). Stir in the chopped nuts. Freeze.

* Yacon syrup and dark (amber) agave impart a nice rich, deep flavor. However, you can use light agave if desired.

** Start with the lesser amount of coconut water and add more as needed.

SOUTHERN CINNAMON PEACH ICE CREAM

Yield 4 servings

1 cup peaches, pitted, chopped and packed

3/4 cup cashews, soaked 1 - 2 hours, drained and rinsed

1/2 cup raw agave nectar or pitted dates, packed

1/4 - 3/4 cup young Thai coconut water, as needed*

1/4 cup young Thai coconut meat

1/4 teaspoon cinnamon

Blend all of the ingredients until smooth and creamy. Freeze.

* Start with the lesser amount of coconut water and add more as needed.

QUICK STRAWBERRY CAROB ICE CREAM

Yield 3 cups

1 1/2 cups fresh strawberries, chopped

3 frozen bananas, chopped

2 tablespoons raw carob powder

2 tablespoons water

Blend everything together (quickly). Don't blend the mixture too long, because you want it like soft-serve ice cream... not a smoothie.

CHOCOLATE HAZELNUT ICE CREAM

Yield 4 - 5 servings

1/4 - 1 cup water, as needed to get everything blending*

1/2 cup hazelnuts, soaked 8 hours, drained and rinsed

1 1/2 cups cashews, soaked 1 - 2 hours, rinsed and drained

1/2 cup raw chocolate powder or raw carob powder

1/2 cup raw dark agave nectar or yacon syrup**

1/2 cup hazelnuts, chopped

Blend all of the ingredients, except the chopped hazelnuts, until smooth and creamy. Just before freezing, stir in the chopped hazelnuts.

* Start with the lesser amount of water and add more as needed. Freeze.

** Dark (or amber or blue) raw agave nectar imparts a deeper, sweet flavor, but you can use raw light agave nectar.

COCONUT PINEAPPLE ICE CREAM

Yield 4 - 5 servings

1 cup cashews, unsoaked

1/4 - 1 cup young Thai coconut water, as needed*

meat of 1 young Thai coconut

1/2 cup fresh pineapple juice

1/2 cup raw agave nectar

2 tablespoons dried coconut, shredded & unsweetened

Grind the nuts in your food processor, with the "S" blade, until coarsely ground. Transfer to a blender and blend all of the ingredients until smooth and creamy.

* Start with the lesser amount of coconut water and add more as needed. Freeze.

RAW VEGAN BANANA SPLITS!

See color photo at KristensRaw.com/photos.

Yield 4 servings

The Main Components

> Sweet Raw Vegan Vanilla Ice Cream (recipe below)
> Sweet Strawberry Coulis (recipe below)
> Raw Velvet Chocolate Sauce (recipe below)
> 1/4 – 1/2 cup chopped walnuts
> 1/4 cup fresh pineapple minced

Sweet Raw Vegan Vanilla Ice Cream

Yield approximately 3 cups

> 1 cup raw cashews
> 1 cup raw macadamia nuts
> 1 cup water
> 4 dates, pitted, soaked 30 minutes, drained
> 1/2 cup raw agave nectar
> 1 whole vanilla bean, minced

Grind the nuts in a food processor, fitted with the "S" blade, until coarsely ground. Place the ground nuts, with the remaining ingredients, in a blender and blend well. Freeze.

Sweet Strawberry Coulis

Yield 1 1/2 cups

    1 (10 oz) bag frozen strawberries, thawed
    1/4 cup raw agave nectar

Blend the ingredients until smooth. After making your banana splits, store any extra coulis in your refrigerator for up to one week. It's a great addition to any smoothie.

Raw Velvet Chocolate Sauce

Yield 3/4 cup

    1/2 cup raw agave nectar
    1/2 teaspoon vanilla extract
    1 tablespoon extra virgin coconut oil
    1/2 teaspoon almond extract
    3 tablespoons raw chocolate powder
    pinch Himalayan crystal salt

Blend all of the ingredients until smooth. After using some on your banana splits, store any left over sauce (to drizzle on top of fresh fruit, or to enjoy by the spoonful) in an airtight glass-mason jar in your refrigerator for up to three weeks.

The Assembly

For each serving, place three small scoops of Sweet Raw Vegan Vanilla Ice Cream on a plate or in a bowl. Top one scoop on each plate with the Sweet Strawberry Coulis, top another one with the Raw Velvet Chocolate Sauce, and top one with the minced pineapple. Then, put the chopped nuts across all of them.

SEXED UP SPICY FROZEN FUDGE BITES

Yield 2 cups to pour into ice cube trays

These won't freeze completely because of the salt, so when you take them out of the ice cube tray, they'll be nice and cold, with a little softness so you can bite right into them, while experiencing a warming sensation from the cayenne. They're "sexy hot" and decadent.

    1/2 cup water

    2 avocados, pitted and peeled

    3/4 cup raw agave nectar

    3/4 cup raw chocolate powder

    1 teaspoon vanilla extract

    approximately 1-2 teaspoons cayenne pepper, or more

    approximately 1-2 teaspoons Himalayan crystal salt granules or more*

Blend the water, avocados, agave, chocolate powder and vanilla until smooth and creamy. Take a pinch of the cayenne pepper and sprinkle it in the bottom of each ice cube partition. Pour in some of the mousse. Then, top each fudge cube with a sprinkle of the salt. Freeze.

* You can use a fine grind here, but I like the bigger granules because it's a salty-sweet-spicy treat and this helps the salt component stand out.

CHAPTER 4

SAUCES, COULIS & GLAZES

The best sauces, or "coulis" (pronounced *"koo-lee"*) for a fancier name, are to simply blend fresh or frozen fruit with a sweetener such as fresh dates or raw agave nectar. Here are some delicious recipes to get you started. I love having these sauces and coulis drizzled over fresh organic fruit or a beautiful slice of Raw cheesecake. They're also great to dip Raw cookies into.

BLACK FOREST SAUCE

Yield 2 1/2 cups

  3/4 cup water

  2 avocados, pitted and peeled

  3/4 cup raw agave nectar or pitted dates, packed

  3/4 cup raw chocolate powder or raw carob powder

  1 teaspoon cherry extract

Serving suggestion for two:

- 2 cups fresh or frozen cherries (1 cup for each serving)

Blend all of the ingredients, except the cherries, until creamy. Drizzle Black Forest Sauce over the cherries and enjoy this rich, sin-free dessert. Store leftover Black Forest Sauce in your refrigerator in an airtight glass mason jar for up to three days to be enjoyed over more fruit or simply by the spoonful.

CAROB GLAZE

Yield approximately 2 cups

Use this fabulous and easy recipe with fresh fruit or add a tablespoon of it to your nut milk or smoothie. It's also perfect on top of Raw vegan ice cream. Or, simply enjoy it by the spoonful!

2 young Thai coconuts (meat and water)
1/2 cup raw agave nectar
1/2 cup raw carob powder

Blend all of the ingredients in a blender until smooth.

LEMON CURD GLAZE

Yield approximately 1 cup

This recipe reminds me of lemon curd, which is a soft and creamy, spreadable cream that has a wonderful and refreshing lemon flavor. It was traditionally used as a spread for scones but nowadays you find it used as a filling for tarts and cakes. This recipe is perfect drizzled over fresh fruit or granola.

1 cup *Crème Fraiche* (see recipe, Chapter 1)
3 tablespoon fresh lemon juice
2 teaspoon fresh grated lemon zest

Simply mix all the ingredients in a bowl by hand. This freezes well.

SMOOTH BLUEBERRY SAUCE

Yield 1 1/2 cup

This is so delicious and stunningly beautiful drizzled over Raw vegan cheesecake. Heck, I like to eat it just as it is, thinking of a sweet summer soup!

2 cups fresh or frozen blueberries
1/3 cup raw agave nectar

Blend all of the ingredients in a blender.

Variation:

- Use any delicious berry for this sauce. Some of my favorites are strawberry, blackberry, mango, peach, and raspberry.

SUPER STAR VANILLA SAUCE

Yield approximately 1 1/2 cups

You just might drink this concoction straight out of the blender it's so "$!@* delicious. Or, you can use this fabulous recipe on fresh organic fruit, Raw ice cream, Raw cheesecake, or add some into a nut milk or smoothie.

1 young Thai coconut (water and meat)

2 tablespoons raw agave nectar

1/2 teaspoon vanilla extract

Blend all of the ingredients in a blender until smooth.

Variations:

- If you'd like a thicker cream for this, just use less coconut water and/or add more coconut meat.
- Add any flavor of extract for more fun and variety. Some of my clients' favorites are coffee, lemon, cherry or peppermint.

VIBRANT BERRY COULIS

Yield 1 1/2 cups

Eat this as is, I'm serious. It's so yummy.

2 cups berries, any fresh or frozen organic mix

1/3 cup soft dates, pitted and packed

Blend all of the ingredients in a blender until you reach your desired texture.

Serving suggestions:

- Put this on top of Raw vegan ice cream or drizzled over a Raw vegan cheesecake, cookie, cake or brownie
- Use this as a dressing on salads or as a dipping sauce for fresh organic fruit

DELECTABLE APRICOT SAUCE

Yield 1 3/4 cups

> 6 - 8 fresh apricots, pitted and chopped
>
> 1/2 cup soft dates, pitted
>
> 1/3 cup fresh orange juice
>
> 1 teaspoon freshly grated orange zest

Puree the apricots and dates in a food processor, fitted with the "S" blade. Add the orange juice and orange zest and process until combined.

SWEET ROSE SAUCE

Yield approximately 1/2 cup

This sauce is great for both sweet dessert and savory vegetable dishes. It's probably not something you'd eat by itself, in my opinion, so when tasting it after you prepare it, make sure to taste it with the fruit or vegetable that it'll be served with. For a worldly experience, try this drizzled over chopped red onions and other vegetables.

> 1/2 cup soft dates, pitted, packed
>
> 2 tablespoons fresh lemon juice
>
> 2 - 3 teaspoons rose water, depending on the strength of rose flavor you desire*
>
> 1/2 cup water, more if desired

In a food processor, fitted with the "S" blade, puree the dates with the lemon juice and rose water, adding enough water to make a creamy sauce.

* You can find rose water at most Middle Eastern markets, online, and at some Whole Foods Markets.

SWEET CASHEW CREAM CHEESE FROSTING

Yield 2 cups

This is great as a frosting for Raw vegan cakes and cookies, and it's simply divine as a dip for fresh, ripe organic fruit.

> 1 1/2 cups cashews, soaked 20 - 30 minutes, drained and rinsed
>
> 3/4 cup *Nourishing Rejuvelac* (see recipe, Chapter 1)
>
> 1/4 cup + 2 tablespoons raw agave nectar
>
> 1 tablespoon extra virgin coconut oil
>
> 1/2 teaspoon almond or vanilla extract

Blend the cashews and rejuvelac in your blender until smooth and wonderfully creamy, adding more rejuvelac if necessary to get it blending.

Optional and recommended step: Pour this mixture (the cashews and rejuvelac) into a fine mesh strainer, and allow it to strain into a bowl. Cover with a damp piece of cheesecloth. Let ferment 10 - 12 hours on your countertop. After cheese has fermented, transfer to a blender and add the remaining ingredients (the agave, coconut oil, and extract). Blend briefly.

OR... bypass the fermenting step and blend in the other ingredients right away. Sweet Cashew Cream Cheese Frosting will last for up to 1 week when stored in an airtight container in the refrigerator. This recipe freezes well.

PEPPERMINT CHOCOLATE SAUCE

Yield approximately 2 cups

Here I go again... I just can't help myself. I adore the peppermint and chocolate flavors. ☺ I will enjoy this delectable sauce by itself (by the spoonful works for me!), as a dip for fresh organic fruit or Raw cookies, or on top of Raw cakes, brownies, and cheesecakes.

    2 young Thai coconuts (meat and water)
    1/2 cup raw agave nectar
    1/4 cup raw chocolate powder
    1/2 teaspoon peppermint extract

Blend all of the ingredients in a blender until smooth and creamy.

Printed in the United States
215009BV00006B/3/P